Root-a-Toot

A Phonics Reader

By Sasha Quinton

The Book Shop, Ltd.

New York, New York

© 2009 The Book Shop, Ltd
Photographs © Juniperimages Corporation

"**Boo-hoo,**" said Panda Cub,
"I'm tired of the **zoo!**

"All I **do** is **snooze** and eat.
I want something **new to do!**"

"**Yoo-hoo,**" said cub's **zoo** friends.
"There's **oodles you** can **do!**

"**You** should make a **goofy** show!
Your friends will all help **you.**"

A big **mule** sang a silly **tune.**
"**Hoo-hoo!**" said the **cockatoo.**

A lion banged on his **new** drum.
A panda **blew** on his **kazoo**.

Penguins dressed in **costumes.**
Two puppies put on **suits.**

An old dog wore a **hula** skirt.
A zebra tried on fancy **boots.**

A turtle rode a skateboard.
A tiger jumped **through hoops.**

Zoom!
Vroom!

Two raccoons danced a **goofy** jig.
A small **goose** skated round in **loops.**

A **baboon** rode a **choo-choo** train.
Then a **cougar** jumped in, **too.**

woo

A **kangaroo** got in the **caboose.**
Two monkeys **hooted** "**Woo-woo-woo!**"

An elephant **stood** on a great big ball.
A giraffe **blew** up a **blue balloon.**

Two pretty **poodles** juggled **fruit,**
And a parrot **flew** right to the **moon.**

"**Yahoo!**" cried Cub, "This show's a **hoot!**"
And he joined them all, singing "**Root-a-toot-toot!**"

Root-
a-toot-
toot